This,

Inu

is for Virginia and Ian

from

Simon Williams

Simon Williams

All best wishes

Oversteps Books

First published in 2016 by　　Oversteps Books Ltd
6 Halwell House
South Pool
Nr Kingsbridge
Devon
TQ7 2RX
UK

www.overstepsbooks.com

Copyright © 2016 Simon Williams
ISBN 978-1-906856-65-6

Printed in Great Britain by imprint digital, Devon

To Jo and the 52 group,
without whom many of these poems
wouldn't have been written or knocked into shape

Acknowledgements

A Portrait of the Lady Elizabeth Oxenham was highly
commended in the Gladstone Library Competition, 2014.
Galileo Galilei was highly commended in the Fire River Poets
competition, 2014.
You Know How Sleep Has a Smell was shortlisted in the
Teignmouth Poetry Competition, 2015.

Poems in this manuscript have appeared in the following
publications:
52 anthology, Nine Arches Press; Acumen; Clear Poetry; Slow
Things anthology, Emma Press; Excite Anthology, 2013, 2014
and 2015; The Forward Book of Poetry, 2015; Hedgerow; I Am
Not a Silent Poet; poetry card commission, Mercedes Benz; The
Plymouth Herald, Poetry 24; Poetry Society (website); In Protest
anthology, Human Rights Consortium; Love and Ensuing
Madness anthology, Rat's Ass Review; Poems for a Liminal Age
anthology, SPM; The Stare's Nest; Three Drops From the
Cauldron; Tribe.

Contents

Trajectory

Imagine an orrery, one of those Victorian
clockworks with all the planets rotating
in their pre-determined ratios.
Imagine that device, held by
an assembly robot, as it works in
independent axes to weld car body panels
to a fraction of a millimetre.

Seat the robot in a roller coaster,
the screwiest at Alton Towers or Disney.
Place the whole ride on an aircraft carrier
in a gale with seas like Robert Garnham's hair.
Position yourself as a spider on brass Neptune
and you're still way short of the course
of Earth, as it burns towards Andromeda.

Messing with the Fruit

I've made a table orrery
with a bright yellow grapefruit at the centre,
a damson for Jupiter, satsuma Saturn.
Closest to the sun, I've put a whortleberry.
I'm pleased with cherry Mars, lychee Venus
have found an ugli fruit for Neptune.
Uranus suits a fig suits Uranus.
Pluto is a Skittle, cast down as not a true fruit.

That leaves Earth.

I've scanned the shelves in Sainsbury's,
been through their guavas and pomegranates.
I asked a greengrocer's advice,
said I wanted something blue and green,
with a soft bloom that scuds across its surface,
something the dew runs round endlessly
to keep fresh, a fruit still on the vine.
He says we need to go organic.

Merchants

Under the Butterwalk,
Peter sells remaindered books
on paper planes, harlequins,
photographs of Cuban cars.
He sits behind his counter, reading,
as his customers browse
their way round to him.

Josie arranges quartz geodes,
malachite, amethyst, tourmaline.
She keeps shelves so full, children
gasp at the shapes of light,
She has two shutters on the crystal shop
which roll down like an old bureau's.

Steve keeps vintage tins,
veteran flat irons, mirrors.
His lurcher curls under a table,
like a grey-haired dragon.
He sells retro to all-comers,
whoever he can tempt in.

Amanda runs the costume museum,
from crinolines to shifts;
the shed coats of party animals.
She lives on-site, doesn't suffer
fools gladly, is none too keen
on bright folk, either.

Under the Butterwalk
nobody sells butter, but sometimes,
when she's pulled the shutters,
Josie swears she can hear,
in the snicket between her
and the French café, the sound
of a nameless cheese, rolling.

Aldershot

Yes, I remember Aldershot –
the name, because one afternoon
of heat the Heathrow coach stopped there
unexpectedly. It was inopportune.

The door released, someone's iPod hissed,
few left or came; it was a comfort stop.
In the bare bus station, what I saw
was a departure board with Aldershot on top

and nettles, shepherd's purse, couch grass,
cow-parsley and some others with long stems.
A man with goggles and a petrol strimmer
was taking out the worst of them.

And for that minute a seagull squawked
close by and then, like some round trip,
further and further, all the gulls
from town centre, way out to the council tip.

Making Fun

When we told Irish jokes, it's said
the Irish told of the Kerry man
and in Kerry they told of the men
of a small village near the sea.

In that village, one bar in particular
took the butt of all their gags
and in that bar, one man, sat at the end,
who once said something foolish.

Spinning and Weaving

Among her many attributes, she appreciated cloth,
the tiny patterns in the warp and weft,
the interlocking 'v's in black and grey and white and brown.
She bought a loom and set it up to weave,
ran the shuttle to and fro like an indecisive mouse,
soon ran out of the sample wools in the box.

He had long kept sheep; Jacobs, at once the dumbest
and the most intelligent, sheared them when the sky was right,
sold fleeces for the price of the ride to market.
He bought a spinning wheel for the corner of his hut,
washed the wool and learnt to spin, careful not to prick
his finger. Finished up with yarn in many natural colours.

She searched wholesalers after she checked her dating site,
where she looked for those with arcane interests in wool,
particularly spinning, weaving and garment-making.

He put a card up in the café window, wanting outlets
for the many skeins of wool he'd spun. He promised
to deliver far over the hills, for the right customer.

Like Water

I have seen the plate,
a thin sheet of titanium
perforated at the edges
for screws to fit it
to a fine, small skull.

It looked like a map;
a section through
that part of the world
I have to look up
for any familiarity.

Between the white teeth
of the Hindu Kush,
the Swat is uncompromised,
moves away, joins other rivers,
each day finds the sea.

The photos are small,
but I can see the way it shines,
Malala, the way it pushes
at the banks when spring comes
with the swell of meltwater.

For Malala Yousafzai, the young Pakistani girl who was shot in the head by Taliban gunmen as she campaigned to promote education for girls. She received reconstructive surgery at Queen Elizabeth Hospital, Birmingham.

'You know how sleep has a smell'

how smells bring back people,
how people have those eyes?

You know how eyes are marbles,
how marbles run along the lines in playgrounds,
how playgrounds are first love?

You know how first love has dinosaurs,
how dinosaurs nearly didn't die,
how death is a change in the weather?

You know how weather has trousers,
how trousers, coats and snoods attract winter,
how winter is the physics of orbit?

You know how orbits bring you round,
how circles have no doors,
how doors are often magnolia?

You know how magnolia has a smell,
how smells bring back people,
often, when you sleep?

Meeting Ivan

Ivan the horse is wary;
he backs away from the gate.
It may be my demeanour,
the remnants of anger,
possibly my orange shirt.

Ivan paws the ground
with his hoof, snorts.
Esther says he's had enough
of the field, wants out
to his stable and the chickens.

The flies are a nuisance
Ivan could do without.
I know how he feels,
though my nose is shorter
so fewer settle.

Ivan has a blaze
between his eyes, not
a perfect diamond, just
a white mark. I have one, too,
slowly subsiding.

Afterlife

When I die,
when all the strange entanglements
of matter rework themselves, maybe just a
hydrogen or two I borrowed for a flick of time
will twist into sea wrack, kapok, coatimundi,
or be blown by the interstellar winds
into the space between things.

Before the universe declines
these atoms could be swirled
into a new, though never new, gas cloud,
be recombined into another star.
Those elements saw the start,
are in me in this serendipity,
will be part of how it ends.

The Host of the Last Supper

It was a troublesome meal. He got rather preachy
and Peter, for one, was confused by the foot washing.
But things got really freaky with the bread and wine;
he tried to make out it was his body and blood.

Now I can see a metaphor as well as the next fisherman
and he seemed convinced he wouldn't be around long,
but even as an allegory, it was beyond strange.
If I'm going to take on board the spirit of God,

I'd rather not pop him in my mouth, piece by piece
and wash it down with a mug of his blood.
I think I can be filled with just a thought of him
anytime I sit in the hills or walk by the sea.

Still, the wine was good, rich as from the highest vineyard,
which in itself was odd, as I set out jugs of water.

Pope Joan Apologises for the Dung Chair

There's a persistent rumour that papal candidates have to be
checked for gender by sitting on a commode-like 'dung chair'.
A Cardinal feels the candidate's genitals and, if found male,
declares 'Duos habet et bene pendentes' or 'He has two, and
they hang well'.

I won't apologise for being Pope. I earned it
fair and square and the costumes were to die for.
Eat well and make pronouncements,
who would baulk at that?

If you believe me, I was quite the polymath;
liberal arts, the scriptures, few could better me.
I had a cardinal, too; still I'll not reveal his name.
He was quite the roly polymath.

I did very little harm. So little Jan Hus argued
the Church could do without a Pope,
as it managed quite well with me. Rat.
My papacy ended at birth.

Many, now, would have me fiction; I didn't make
the Oxford Dictionary of Popes, but in Rome
they weren't so very sure. The tale twisted
like a corkscrew at an All Saints' feast.

I will say sorry for the dung chair;
no one likes a strange prelate at their privates.
Plenty tried with me, only one succeeded.
He had two, they dangled nicely.

Galileo Galilei

I can see the fortifications of Santa Rosita, Signor Galilei.

Of course you can, you old fool,
you're looking through a telescope.
You could use it to watch the young girls
brush out their hair in La Frezzeria bedrooms
or point it up to see the *Tre Cime di Lavardo*
far off in the mountains, but better,
you could, with the right inclination,
see such details of the six bright spheres,
you would be perfectly astonished.

You could see the phases of our sister Venus,
the way Saturn is haloed, Mars cross-hatched,
the swirling eye that stares from Jupiter's head
and even, though I'm still recording,
can't confirm my lenses have detected it,
a new planet, small and far out from the centre,
a watery, icy place, cold as Poseidon.
You could see all this, and if your head
weren't full of banquets and crystal rings,
conclude we're all of us, God willing,
rotating slowly round the Sun.

The first line is spoken by The Doge of Venice in Galileo Galilei *by Bertholt Brecht.*

Daniel Defoe Assesses the Great Storm, 1703

Now the full toll is beginning to be read,
London has a potency of hurt; lead from St Paul's,
chimneys by the hundred.
The good Queen's taken to the cellars of St James'.

The third-rate (battleship) HMS Stirling Castle
was wrecked on the Goodwin Sands.
70 men, including four marine officers,
were saved, but 206 men were drowned.

Samuel has ridden down from Cambridge,
says King's College boys have not escaped.
Pinnacles have pitched and tumbled through the roof.
Many sent down.

The sixth-rate advice boat Eagle
was lost on the coast of Sussex,
but her ship's company of 45
were all saved.

Admiral Sir Cloudesley Shovell, if I believe the man,
had his vessel blown from Harwich to Gothenburg,
all across the sea, before he could
get wind of her and steer her home.

The fourth-rate Newcastle
was lost at Spithead.
The carpenter and 39 men were saved,
and the other 193 were drowned.

Good Bishop Kidder and his wife –
I met them once, were taken in their bed in Wells,
by chimneys off the palace.
The great west window shattered like bone.

The third-rate Resolution *was lost at Pevensey*
on the coast of Sussex;
all her ship's company of 221
were saved.

In the level lands of Somerset, a new ocean,
archipelagos of farms and villages.
Families taken, men stranded;
pitched up like castaways.

The fourth-rate Reserve *was lost*
by foundering off Yarmouth. The captain, the surgeon,
the clerk and 44 men were saved;
the other 175 members of the crew were drowned.

Henry Winstanley, who had a way with water,
was in his lighthouse on the Eddystone,
waiting for the 'Greatest Storm'. both tower and man
enveloped; their candles dowsed.

The italicised passages are part of an Admiralty report on the results of the
Great Storm.

A Portrait of the Lady Elizabeth Oxenham

Lord

This salon needs a portrait of Elizabeth, to outshine
all my piebald, wholesome, pompous ancestry,
but she insists on posing in that russet, lampas gown
and holding to a Jincheng from the orangery.

Then there's that rotten whippet, though I suppose
I shouldn't blame the hound, he has been spoilt
by the rigours of the sitting room. She has him on the chaise,
feeds him titbits, by night he lies out on her quilt.

I wouldn't mind his situation, if I could lie out under it
and have the lustful lady under me, but like
an English baker, she picks bloomers, not baguette
leaves me stroking crumbs and long awake.

Whippet

I've always thought her far the better of the two;
he barely pays me any heed, except when coursing,
while she, at least and often, out of the blue,
fondles my ears, chucks my chin, as if rehearsing

strokes and little pettings she imagines.
When we sit before the fire, of an evening,
she talks as though I'm more than hound companion.
I crawl a little closer on the sofa, scent her breathing,

listen to her eyes, taste her fingers on my haunch.
She talks, but never says my name (like I'm homunculus),
in such sweet tones, I'm sure she'd wrench
the heart of any troubadour, but not that anus.

Lady

He has his uses. I admit I found him gallant
when first we rode out, him on his starred stallion,
but even at our first reception, I saw his talent
to wear medals on his chest, with me his new medallion.

Oh, the boredom of this place, its nail-clipped hedges,
dead echoes in the rooms, the powder-boy footmen.
I took his name and all the hidden pledges –
like him in bed; the fallen ox of the Oxenhams.

This portrait he commissioned is of him as much as me:
his dog, his fruit, materials he dressed me in.
My only solace is Mr Kneller's brush, its tip and belly,
his tented smock, my flip-up merkin.

Operators of the Puffing Devil

*Richard Trevithick's first steam-powered road vehicle caught fire and
was ruined after it was left by its operators in a gully, while they
went for dinner.*

I wasn't saying he was crazy;
it was a prime thing and I could see its worth,
carrying people up Camborne Hill
like half a dozen horses.

I *would* say its wheels were thin,
more like a cart's than an engine's.
To take that weight, a bit of spread
would have stopped them making runnels.

When we ran that gulley, I never
thought we'd make it out again
and Arthur was a bit lam-handed
with the steering and the throttle.

There's no way we could move it
once stuck there in the hollow
and it was getting late and us pair
devilish hungry. We went to eat

and no-one could begrudge us that,
though looking back on it, we prob'ly
should have doused the firebox first.
We went over to the Skinner's and had goose.

A good roast bird it was and as we ate,
I said *Now that's a real machine:
no steam, no ratchets, cams nor valves
and one as can go on water, earth*

*and air with equal versatility.
It'll take a while for Dick Trevithick
to better that one ... and to give it taste.*
We finished with a quart of ale, before the fire.

Strong Arms for Armstrong

Swimming can hurt your arms in May,
when the water's cold and you spend
each 40 minute lesson elbow-locked
on the grab-rail, a toy acrobat
permanently squeezed to the top.

In July, when the sun had warmed
the pool and we splashed like
netted herring in the shallow end,
Miss Armstrong hauled us to the side,
commanded us to swim widths.

Some, with paddles dogs would scorn,
made it to the other rail, most gave out
around the middle of The Great Expanse.
After, as we dried, I boasted it was just
the others splashing stopped me.

Go on then, on your own. Get in.
Arms V-ed back on the rail, a kick
a frog prince could have claimed,
several strokes we'll call freestyle and
I touched the far side. There was applause.

Stations on the Metropolitan Line

Last night Simon Armitage and another poet whose name I knew earlier this morning brought me a garden for my living room. Obviously a gift, I couldn't object to the swathe of tall grasses in pots that covered the old, patchy, fawn carpet, but in the kitchen there were two railway carriages and another in the small back garden: each a different type, a different era, not models. Funny how a new arrival can trigger memory, of Chalfont and Latimer, as I went to school each day and the diesel cars mixed with the Metropolitan line, the silver Underground, their automatic doors closing out each station. Even then, there was the occasional 2-6-0, pulling an express from Aylesbury or Oxford, and sometimes a small diesel traction unit, like something from Switzerland, but without the pantographs, pulling carriages of properly dressed commuters and, possibly, Betjeman heading for the BBC.

Threes and Fives

We were warned against *The Wall*;
a pub where undergrads weren't welcome,
a pub for the workers from Brush Lighting.
One door, one small casement;

you could see where the name came from.
One bar with two pumps: bitter and mild,
Walkers crisps in the three flavours.
The publican pulled two pints without a word.

We asked for dominoes from a stack of wooden sets.
We had mastered the rules of Threes and Fives
but not the strategy. No simple matching up –
this was Men's Dominoes.

Two blokes came over from a table by the window.
Want to play pairs? they asked.
We shuffled the tiles round and round;
each took seven: three in left hand, four in right.

Twelve for four; they moved the cribbage peg.
We responded *Six for two*, but *Nine for three*.
After twenty five plays and three knocks,
they were pegged up ten at the end of the hand.

System Mechanics, Materials Science could do little,
nor countless hands of bridge in sixth-form common rooms.
Just knowing how to play the game, counted;
four/one in hands by the end of half an hour.

Engineer covers all kinds of work with blocks and studs.
They said, *Shuffle 'em again, lads. We'll get beers in.*

Buns

When she was young,
Susan used to feed
the hippos at London Zoo
with current buns.

She'd toss them up
in a neat arc to land
on their huge tongues,
between the two stump teeth.

Later, the zoo put up signs
Do not feed the hippopotami.
Their natural diet
is grasses and weed.

Susan said, *The buns never*
seemed to do them any harm.
The hippos said,
What are buns made from?

The Best Time of Night

That time, at three in the morning, you woke me, said you
wanted sex and the milk-light of the moon filled the room
like a three Watt daylight bulb and I was awake then, as most
men would be, and we threw the duvet off and, as near to
abandoned as we may ever get, we lay and kissed and licked
and stroked and curled tongues round and in and out of
most parts we could find (did I mention the moonlight?)
and what I couldn't reach with tongue we let my cock explore
and it proved capable enough, which isn't boasting,
so you squeezed and I pushed and in the end it took
our breath away, not just the squeezing, but the warmth
and slippage, the wrinkling of the sheets and the shadow
of the hair on your lower belly, like a forest on the moon.

How We Fit into the Scheme of Things

It has been a good universe.
Most of it went as planned;
a few nebulae out of place,
a shortfall of proper intelligence.

We walked out around the lake,
as flat as fresh ice; the only ripples
from a stream off the moor,
channelling last week's rain.

That little place, third out
from its paltry star; they had
a few good ideas: buttons,
sherbet dib-dabs, love.

It was good the day the tide
missed our fast-discarded clothes
and the sand didn't grind us away.
The sun tanned my back, your front.

They never really got along,
always squabbled about silly things.
It was better when the octopuses
came to prominence; such dexterity.

I remember you at birth, twice;
their looks of surprise, their heads
of hair, how quick you came
to them with milk and cradling.

So often the hominids and cephalopods
had the right idea; their scientists were
bright. If only they had given more time
to the poets, particularly the cuttlefish.

A Humanist Notes a Coincidence

i.m. Ellie Davies

After an evening
celebrating
the life of a
fine poet,
newly dead,

we drive from
Abergavenny
to Monmouth,
through the
dogged night.

At this time
a small rock,
possibly the size
of a brain or a heart
enters the air.

Rather than skipping
the atmosphere,
as on a pond,
it drops straight
down to earth.

We see it
as a white
streak, an
exclamation
mark

!

Dive

You can tell it's a dive 'cos the carpet is sticky.
The beer is Korean on a corporate tab.
When you don't know the district, you can't be too picky.

The pool table's bald, the balls none too clicky
and one of them's missing — still, we'll give it a stab.
You can tell it's a dive 'cos the cues are both sticky

and the music's all 70s, kicked off with *Ricky
Don't Lose That Number*, now something more drab.
When you don't know the language, you can't be too picky.

Casses all round and, just to be gimmicky,
a shot for the loser – tequila's the jab.
You can tell it's a dive 'cos the shot glass is sticky,

the lemon is tasteless, the spirit is tricky,
they've seen that we're foreign with money to nab.
When you don't know the hustle, you can't be too picky.

The music gets louder, just time for a quickie;
it'll soon be the moment to call us a cab.
You can tell it's a dive, 'cos the clock hands are sticky;
if you don't know the hour, they've slipped you a mickey.

from dream

The First Time Ever I Kissed Kate Bush

was last night,
in some old lecture hall,
perhaps an Oxford College. Jesus.

I don't recall
what the event was –
sitting next to Kate Bush, you wouldn't.

She looked young,
probably all the dancing
and running up hills.

Remembering Kate
doesn't discuss her family life,
we talked of music and movements:

red shoes, kangaroos,
the contemplation of Pi,
what she'd been up to in the last 35 years.

The others filed out.
It was going really well,
till at last Kate had to leave.

The kiss was unexpected,
so slightly fumbled at the start,
but there were tongues.

Margin Notes

I wandered lonely as a sheep
That trips on high o'er vales and hills,
When all at once I saw a crowd,
A host of little whippoorwills.

When I am an old woman I shall wear leather
And a chipped crash hat with a purple flash
And I shall spend my pension on studded gloves and beer
And an old Harley and say we've no money for butter

They help you out, you mum and dad,
They want to do their best, they do.
They try to hide the faults they have
And leave a clean slate, just for you.

Nobody heard him, the fat man,
But still he lay, snoring.
I was in the shallows, splashing about
And not swimming, but paddling.

Pike, three inches long, perfect
Pike in all parts, green tigering the gold
Killers from the egg: the malevolent aged grin
They dance on the surface among the flies
And their little fins glitter in the sparkly sun.

Needs something more fluffy, more solitary than sheep, I think. Also, not sure about the whippoorwills. Perhaps I should set it in the lakes, like the others.

Wonder if this is over the top? Want to be eccentric, without being too 'biker'. Would clashing colours be enough?

This is crap. It's got no bite. My parents fucked me up — can I get away with that?

Needs more drama. Don't like 'snoring' — it's too joyful. Could I be out of my depth?

This rings true to me, though I could perhaps lose the last line.

Filaments

She allows nothing bigger than nail clippers
and, I ask you, what good are they with this
much of it? – like crossing the Atlantic with flippers
and no boat. The wonder is it's not just frizz

after this time. I spend hours washing, combing,
picking things from it: bugs, brambles, bellbine,
the occasional prince – it brings them like homing
pigeons, though they're not as tasty. It's fine

for you to laugh at this point, my little joke,
not so the length of my incarceration.
There's more to life than hooks and hair, oak
and elm, the girth of my accommodation.

I'll have to get back to you; it sounds as though
another pigeon prince is cooing, down below.

Spoiler Alert

Within this jug there is good liquor;
'Tis fit for parson or for vicar,
But how to drink and not to spill
Will try the utmost of your skill.

The trick to drink is not to tip it;
hard, because to gulp or sip it,
it's natural to lift to lip. It
then just spills on man or whippet.

Instead, put thumb and finger on its
two small spouts around the bonnet.
Put lips on third and suck upon it,
but just get air; the jug's a con. Its

handle needs a final grommet;
thumb it. Drink deep. End this sonnet.

Based on Puzzle Jug, Royal Albert Memorial Museum, Exeter, Gallery 4,
Item 4. First stanza is inscription on jug.

Shades

They had us stabbing sacks,
running up and thrusting – like loading hay.
I was good at it, always liked building stooks,
but we were gutting them.
What have I done, Amy? All the village took to us
when we signed up for the sergeant: John and Ned,
George and Henry Buttercombe.

Now, the boys, all of them, though barely one will say,
wonder if the French are worth it.
Weren't we killing them at Waterloo?
Next week we ship out to Étaples,
will be at the front, they say, by Friday.
Will you walk me through your father's wood:
oak and elm, willow, chestnut?

Bill, I told you not to do it.
They're not conscripting and you could be reserved,
working on the land. I'll walk you through
the dingle, not that you don't know the way.
I thought, last week, how often we had walked in shade,
with the sun up in the blaze of July,
how easily we turned brown, never carmine red.

Airway Beacons, 1921

By day we use the arrows, 70ft of concrete each,
pointing all the way from San Francisco to New York.
They're set into the Rockies, onto the Great Planes,
through the lowlands, over the Appalachians, every 10 miles.

On a good day, out of twister season, you can see
three or four, like *Cut here* on a coupon.

At night, the beacons on the towers do it, the nearest
flares like the sun, the farthest is a pinprick
you're not sure you can see. It's like looking at the smallest
star from Argo, Alabama, pitched in the ripples of August.

We fly our double-wingers through rain and heat
and gloom of night. Night wins it for me.

I prefer to dead reckon, use Orion's belt buckle, take
a right at the Big Dipper and straight on till morning.
My only passengers are sacks of US Mail, who never
need to land to find a diner, take a leak.

I can fly till the stars fry, eggs over easy, and
night pours into the Hudson like percolated coffee.

Mr Toad's Ode to the Open Road

a Pindaric Ode

There was a time when willow tree and yew,
the river, rowing boat and rod
were all I knew,
protected by some minor god,
who danced on hooves and played the old kazoo.
But now the tune is faint among the reeds,
webs itch to be away
and so today
we'll follow where the dusty tracks and turnpikes lead.

As daybreak's brightening arc
gives life to lamb and lark,
the horse pulls on the staves,
the canary coloured cart rolls on,
even grudging Rat behaves.
The open road, beyond
slow waterway and swallow swoop,
is just the place to meet a marque,
where horseless carriage outshines horse and cart – *poop, poop.*

There was a time when cartwheels, wood and screw
and painted cover made of rag
were all I knew,
directed by some minor nag
who tramped on hooves and clicked a metal shoe.
But now I've seen the rapturous motor car,
I know *that* love was fad.
Now I'm just glad
I'll ever chase its little circled, three-point star.

On a Young Girl and a Chimpanzee Playing Chess

It started in the playground; she'd only be up
to the third rung, while I was sitting
on the frame top. She'd walk the rope bridge,
holding the hand ropes and stepping plank to plank,
while I'd go gibbon-swinging from its underside.

I don't blame her; it's just her strange anatomy.
Those thin fingers and stumpy arms aren't up to it.
Her legs are too long for the trees, as well,
though I look up to her when we walk.
You'd think chess would be her thing.

She opened pawn to king's bishop 3. I played pawn to king 4;
conventional enough, so many games start this way,
but when she followed pawn to king's knight 4,
I thought *Do you really want to do that?*
I contemplated queen to king's rook 4, checkmate,

but her father had had words before we started.
I guess like all of us, he wanted to protect his child,
keep her from another disappointment.
He appealed to my baser instincts, said
Let the kid win; there's a banana in it for you.

Note: the chess moves constitute Fool's Mate.

Inti

was the Inca name for the Sun, which space scientists have now given to a particle of dust collected by the Stardust probe from the Wild 2 (VILT-two) comet.

More universal than stars, planets,
rocks in the Oort cloud, is dust.
The black specks in this Aerogel –

the traces, like meteors
in a Perseid shower – hang on the
wild comet's tail through its ellipses;
no corners to settle into, beyond Jupiter.

Inti is the exotics: magnesium, aluminium,
minerals not formed in the absolute of space,
only near a star, via the heat of its hydrogen.

I sweep the kitchen floor – skin flakes,
leaf skeletons, the grit abraded from tors.
Perhaps, by the chance that orbits suns,
stardust is driven through the bristles of this broom.

Fish House

Imagine a house of plate glass,
four square cavity walls of it,
sealed against the weather.
Fill the gaps with water,
pour in gravel, weighted weeds
and fish, in that order.

Tall thin fish would be the best;
angel fish, sunfish with big spots.
They could only turn round at the corners,
but would have two full stories
to rise and fall in, like a slice through
a shallow, tropical sea.

Blow bubbles from the air-con,
warm in winter, cool in summer.
Contemplate the fish in their tall tank,
free to swim all around the house:
kitchen, bedroom, lounge,
bathroom. The fish could watch you
in your glass bath, underwater.

Star Fish

Lyra worked with fish: Koi carp,
rudd and gudgeon. She fed them
flakes and mealworms, which they
nibbled from her fingers like space dust.

Sometimes, on the odd night shift,
she stood beside the pool and pointed out
the constellations, more as proof of astronomy
than to teach her charges new celestial shapes.

She showed them Pegasus and Fornax,
how the lines of Crux and Lupus fell
across the sky, the way Reticulum
was not a net to frighten them.

On the surface there was no reaction;
they still darted to the weed each time
a shadow fell across the sheeny water,
still breached its tension when the sun shone.

Down below, although to the untrained eye
they only made a 'V' as they shoaled
from end to end, those who understood knew
they'd nearly fathomed out the shape of Pisces.

Dendrogramma Enigmatica

First scraped off the sea floor with a sled,
the creature of the title, like a seahorse parasol,
has mouthparts down its stem
and a many-forked digestive tract
all through its bust-umbrella canopy
(there's a notch in every brolly
which lets the water through).

If it's to be a new phylum,
not species, genus, family, order or class,
but phylum, as researchers claim,
there's just the edging of a wish
that, rather than a minute mushroom animal,
it could have been a gryphon.

On Dolphin Poetry

Of course our poetry is mainly oral,
although one or two experimental pieces
involving the placement of pebbles, shells
and small crustaceans have been tried
by the Language Pods, with varying success.

Before that, most work was seascapes
or about relationship. There is a school of poets
now, though, who are trying to relate
more to the world we see about us,
to inhabit the skins of other creatures.

It's hard, of course, not to be labelled
cetaceomorphic – applying dolphin characteristics
to lesser beings – but there is value, if we can
explore the way they behave, or even reason,
(assuming that verb is not itself impertinence).

I heard a recitation only yesterday;
a celebrated humpback from the Southern seas
trying to get into the mind of a human, move behind
the bizarre squeaking, the inexhaustible
desire to kill. It was thought-provoking,

but in the end, I wonder at the value in it.
Very few dealings with humans have proved helpful.
The few who have a modicum of understanding
are only interested in notation. As I said to
Chkchkchkchkchk, a poem does not float, it flows.

Beautiful

I want to meet the man who drew Maleficent;
it will have been a man, animating those lips, eyes,
Jean Harlow glances, Bette Davis sneers.

I want to meet the man who made her move
without the need to waltz, sliding over the floor
like a Dalek's wet dream.

I want to meet the woman who spoke for her.
Who needs Aurora when you hear
this venom voice? — Voldemort's dominatrix.

There's something of the worst of night about her,
that part when you have checked beneath the bed,
lie back and know all checks are pointless.

Something of the gap between the lightning and the thunder,
you know Tchaikovsky knew as he pitched her there,
thumb and finger poisoning the needle tip.

Fitting Him

The trousers were fine;
a good pair of cream chinos,
some flounce, not cutting him
but slimline, to exploit his figure.

The shirt and jacket
were the problems, I could
see we'd have trouble when
he ducked through the doorway.

He wanted something, he said,
smart casual, not too bright,
friendly, but with a little distance,
good for enunciations.

I puzzled over this;
to me he spoke very clearly,
if a little boomy, slightly
over-authoritarian.

He was one of your
Laura Ashley, William Morris types.
Lovely complexion, a certain glow.
He could almost take a dress.

We tried a number of styles,
different cloths, but really
it was the fit that was amiss.
I told him, I said

I'm sorry, sir, but there's
not much call for your ... irregularities.
Our normal run of customer
is less well-endowed.

As a last resort, I mentioned
Dawkins & Hitchens, Ecclesiastical Outfitters,
thought they might have something
for the wings.

Sneaking an Angel Into a Poem

It was when they drained Venn reservoir
and we could see the undulating gravel at its base.
We walked the tourist track, grown clammy
through the wet weather.

At the small bridge, where a stream runs down
helplessly to trickle charge the lake before the dam,
we looked North East, when Susan said,
Oh My God, an angel.

Sure enough, in the shallows of the water,
not attempting to walk it, as another might,
an angel, its grey glow shimmering this late December,
visited.

We couldn't tell its gender, Uriel or one from Zechariah.
Kit once said he'd always thought they went
straight down like teddy bears, though obviously
without the golden fur.

We stood like shepherds, virgins, ufologists,
neither of us thought to take a mobile to it.
It didn't seem to want to impart secret knowledge,
just fixed a stare towards the bank.

I hear you getting restive, the first vibrations
of complaint, with reference to the title.
It distinctly says '*Sneaking* An Angel
Into A Poem'

Yet this apparition has hardly snuck;
its long, thin legs are placed there, bold as brass.
Its wings, when it should care to use them,
move the real air.

Which only shows the unreliability of poets,
making more of everyday events than they have cause to.
With fresh examination of the facts, as pertinent,
I now believe it was a heron.

On a Handwritten Copy of Ariel

Sent To Al Alvarez By Sylvia Plath

It looks cheery
for all its power,
bold nib on thin paper.

Just what you might write
after a canter to Ivy Tor
as the sky steps to day.

Just what you might write
when you've got
the kids to sleep;

over a Homewheat and tea,
sit down to produce
a fair copy for Al.

Out of the window,
the courtyard,
the lour of hills –

rock teeth:
a lookout and
to chew you up.

Just what you might write
to throw off
old identities.

Just what you might write
to shimmy down
structure.

Not an error,
not a stroke of Tippex
to refine white.

At the bottom,
a small red flower,
perhaps a Cinquefoil,

picked from the marsh.

Pushing it

I know I had the lion's share
of the cheesecake, so there was
no excuse for sneaking the last piece
out of the fridge. It was delicious,
and love means never having to say you're sorry.

I know you wanted to see part three
of that period romp with David Tennant,
but this Eastern Europe grudge match
was just too tempting. There's always iPlayer,
and love means never having to say you're sorry.

I know we agreed you'd have the car today,
but Steve and Joe are celebrating something
and need a designated driver.
I've oiled the chain on your bike,
and love means never having to say you're sorry.

You know that floral print
with the tie-back sleeves I showed you.
I used your PayPal account to buy it.
Lions don't eat cheesecake,
and 'love means never having to say you're sorry'

is bollocks, which, incidentally
you won't be needing tonight.

Wolf Talk

The woman in the church house on the moor
talks of Yellowstone wolves, of the Agate,
Blacktail, Gibbon Meadows packs,
of how they're closer to Pekingese than Husky.
She runs through their hunting sequence:
orient > eye-stalk > chase > grab-bite >
kill-bite > dissect > consume.

The woman in the church house on the moor
speaks of how an adult wolf is trainable,
not tameable, how when first brought home,
it must have been the part-grown juveniles,
with prey drive still developing: orient >
eye-stalk > chase, whose muzzles could be
shaped into those breathless, Beijing faces.

The woman in the church house on the moor
says a wolf is a wolf is a wolf,
that they vary only in the prey they choose,
develop speed for elk or strength for bison.
She says, should you meet a loner in the park,
it will run before you do. Just never meet
the gaze in its age-old, xanthous eyes.

A Wolf Explains the Howl

In his book, The Philosopher and the Wolf, Mark Rowlands
tells how his wolf would sit howling while his mother cooked.
The wolf was asking for cheese, which it loved.

As we sit out under lupine constellations,
lay our heads back, roll our tongues, breathe deep,
we're not calling to our mates, challenging our rivals
we don't do it to integrate the pack.
So few of you have taken time to study,
so few know how we long for Wensleydale
how we lament the lack of Limburger in forests,
yearn for little Edams in the vast, cold tundra.

Why else would we howl so under the full moon?
Even the ponderous trappers know the way it looks.
Don't come with guns to keep your fluffy mutton safe.
Don't send your puny dogs to save your chickens.
In the frozen nights, where all we have for life is what we eat,
bring us cheese. O, bring us cheese.

Trophic Cascade

If you take a dozen wolves
from Saskatchewan or Manitoba,
release them slowly into Yellowstone,

if they eat elk and bison (a few)
start them moving from the
plains to the sides of valleys,

if the grass and trees recover –
aspen, pine and cottonwood –
grow taller, thicker, lay down roots,

if their cover gives chances to
field mice and songbirds, hence
badgers, foxes and coyotes,

if the grasslands recover
and the trees cling on to soil
that might have washed away,

if the river banks are stabilised
and beavers make more pools
for otters, ducks and muskrats,

that's how wolves change
the course of rivers. They call it out
across the whole caldera.

A Selection of Haiku from the Haiku Trolley

japonica falls
the novice traps petals
in her folded letter

police siren
across the traffic jam
nobody moves

written in the sand
where every seventh wave wipes
is the answer to ...

beyond Mars, a comet sings
how did the nightjar
learn its song

we planted privet
and laurel to beat the winds
betting our hedges

few birds sing
a girl goes out to fetch the cows
whistling

Oversteps Books Ltd

The Oversteps list includes books by the following poets:

David Grubb, Giles Goodland, Alex Smith, Will Daunt, Patricia Bishop, Christopher Cook, Jan Farquarson, Charles Hadfield, Mandy Pannett, Doris Hulme, James Cole, Helen Kitson, Bill Headdon, Avril Bruton, Marianne Larsen, Anne Lewis-Smith, Mary Maher, Genista Lewes, Miriam Darlington, Anne Born, Glen Phillips, Rebecca Gethin, W H Petty, Melanie Penycate, Andrew Nightingale, Caroline Carver, John Stuart, Rose Cook, Jenny Hope, Hilary Elfick, Anne Stewart, Oz Hardwick, Terry Gifford, Michael Swan, Maggie Butt, Anthony Watts, Joan McGavin, Robert Stein, Graham High, Ross Cogan, Ann Kelley, A C Clarke, Diane Tang, R V Bailey, John Daniel, Alwyn Marriage, Simon Williams, Kathleen Kummer, Jean Atkin, Charles Bennett, Elisabeth Rowe, Marie Marshall, Ken Head, Robert Cole, Cora Greenhill, John Torrance, Michael Bayley, Christopher North, Simon Richey, Lynn Roberts, Sue Davies, Mark Totterdell, Michael Thomas, Ann Segrave, Helen Overell, Rose Flint, Denise Bennett, James Turner, Sue Boyle, Jane Spiro, Jennie Osborne, John Daniel, Janet Loverseed, Wendy Klein, Sally Festing, Angela Stoner and Susan Taylor.

For details of all these books, information about Oversteps and up-to-date news, please look at our website and blog:

www.overstepsbooks.com
http://overstepsbooks.wordpress.com